Jacob of Sarug's Homilies on the Six Days of Creation: The Second Day

Texts from Christian Late Antiquity

40

Series Editor

George Anton Kiraz

TeCLA (Texts from Christian Late Antiquity) is a series presenting ancient Christian texts both in their original languages and with accompanying contemporary English translations.

Jacob of Sarug's Homilies on the Six Days of Creation: The Second Day

Edited and Translated by

Edward G. Mathews Jr.

gorgias press
2016

Gorgias Press LLC, 954 River Road, Piscataway, NJ, 08854, USA

www.gorgiaspress.com

Copyright © 2016 by Gorgias Press LLC

All rights reserved under International and Pan-American Copyright Conventions. No part of this publication may be reproduced, stored in a retrieval system or transmitted in any form or by any means, electronic, mechanical, photocopying, recording, scanning or otherwise without the prior written permission of Gorgias Press LLC.

2016

ISBN 978-1-4632-0553-9   ISSN 1935-6846

Library of Congress Cataloging-in-Publication Data

```
Names: Jacob, of Serug, 451-521, author. | Matthews,
Edward G., Jr., 1954- |
   Jacob, of Serug, 451-521. Homilies on the six
days of creation. Second
     day. | Jacob, of Serug, 451-521. Homilies on the
six days of creation.
     Second day. English.
Title: Jacob of Serug's Homilies on the six days of
creation. Second day /
     edited and translated by Edward G. Mathews Jr.
Description: Piscataway, NJ: Gorgias Press, 2016. |
Series: Texts from
     Christian late antiquity, ISSN 1935-6846 ; 40 |
Includes bibliographical
     references.
Identifiers: LCCN 2016001269 | ISBN 9781463205539
(Paperback)
Subjects: LCSH: Creation--Sermons. | Sermons,
Syriac. | Sermons,
     Syriac--Translations into English.
Classification: LCC BS651 .J33 2016 | DDC
222/.1106--dc23
LC record available at
http://lccn.loc.gov/2016001269
```

Printed in the United States of America

For my mother
† 26 April 2015
Sunday of the Good Shepherd

ܩܘܡ ܠܟܝ ܪܥܝܬܝ ܫܦܝܪܬܝ
ܚܙܝ ܐܢܐ ܒܗ ܠܟܝ ܒܡܠܟܘܬܐ

TABLE OF CONTENTS

Table of Contents v
Abbreviations vii
Introduction 1
   Outline 1
   Summary 4
Text and Translation 5
   I.   God is first a 'Creator', then a 'Maker' (521–548) 6
   II. The Firmament divided the upper from the lower waters (549–604) 10
   III. The Area above the Firmament is completely still and serene (605–632) 16
   IV. Like the Firmament, Man is placed between the waters (633–660) 18
   V. The Firmament is a roof over this world, the source of night (661–698) 20
   VI. The Firmament was established for the benefit of mankind (699–794) 24
   VII. The Firmament was created incomplete, without sun, stars and moon (795–822) 32
   VIII. Day Two was the first moment in the planned progression of Creation (823–842) 34
Bibliography of Works Cited 39
   Primary Texts 39
      Eusebius of Emesa 39
      Basil 39
      Ephrem 39
      Theodoret of Cyrus 39
      Eghishe 40
      Jacob of Sarug 40
      Narsai 40
   Secondary Works 40

Index of Names and Themes 43
Index of Biblical References 45

ABBREVIATIONS

Bedjan	P. Bedjan, *Homiliae Selectae Mar-Jacobi Sarugensis* (see Bibliography)
BETL	Bibliotheca Ephemeridum Theologicarum Lovaniensium
CBOTS	Coniectanea Biblica. Old Testament Series
CSCO	Corpus Scriptorum Christianorum Orientalium
FOTC	Fathers of the Church
OCA	*Orientalia Christiana Analecta*
OCP	*Orientalia Christiana Periodica*
OS	*L'Orient Syrien*
OtSt	*Oudtestamentische Studien*
PdO	*Parole de l'Orient*
PO	Patrologia Orientalis
S	*Sobornost*
SC	Sources Chrétiennes
TFCLA	Texts from Christian Late Antiquity

INTRODUCTION

> INFORMATION ON THIS HOMILY
> Homily Title: Homily on the Fashioning of Creation, The Second Day
> Source of Text: *Homiliae Selectae Mar-Jacobi Sarugensis*, edited by Paul Bedjan (Paris-Leipzig: Harrassowitz, 1907, 2nd ed. Piscataway: Gorgias Press, 2006), vol. 3, pp. 27–43. [Homily 71b]
> Lines: 322 [521–842]

OUTLINE

As was the case with our previous translation of Day 1,[1] the text translated here is not a complete integral homily. What is here translated rather constitutes the second part of Jacob's very long *Mêmrâ 71: On the Fashioning of Creation*,[2] which is entirely concerned with Day 2 of creation as found in Genesis 1:6–8. The complete *Mêmrâ 71* is the longest of all Jacob's *mêmrê*, far longer than even his famous *Mêmrâ on the Parrot who squawked out the Trisagion*.[3] While a partial English translation of Day 1 had already existed before our complete translation, there are no modern language translations of any other day; thus, this is the first translation of Day 2 from Jacob's *Mêmrâ 71: On the Fashioning of Creation*.

Although it was preceded by Ephrem's *Commentary on Genesis*, which work Jacob clearly follows in his own exposition, this long

---

[1] Mathews, *Jacob of Sarug's Homilies on the Six Days of Creation: The First Day*; it is hoped that the rest will also appear much more quickly than these two fascicules have appeared.

[2] Bedjan, III.1–151; cf. summary and study in T. Jansma, "L'Hexaméron de Jacques de Sarug".

[3] Bedjan, I.84–174.

1

Mêmrâ 71: On the Fashioning of Creation nonetheless constitutes the first Syriac *Hexaemeron*, or commentary on the six days of creation, as set forth in Genesis 1.[4] As such, Jacob's *Mêmrâ 71* occupies a similar position to Basil's *Homilies on the Hexaemeron* in the Greek patristic tradition, which too was preceded by commentaries on Genesis (Origen, Didymus, et al.).[5] Curiously, it was not until the late VIIth or very early VIIIth century before another *Hexaemeron* was composed in either of these two great traditions.[6] While Basil's *Homilies on the Hexaemeron* certainly existed in Syriac translation before Jacob began to compose his *mêmrâ*,[7] there is still no clear evidence that he made any use of it or had even consulted it.

In his discussion of the Genesis account of what was created on the second day as found in the part of *Mêmrâ 71* translated here, Jacob, following the biblical account, exposits on the creation of the firmament: what it was, where it was, what—as far as can be determined—was placed above it and what below it, its purpose and utility for humanity, and the importance of its place in the Genesis account of the six day progression of creation. Jacob uses several words to describe the physical structure of this firmament that covers the entire earth, the "great house of mankind": tent

---

[4] Although, technically, Jacob's *mêmrâ* is a *Heptaemeron*, as the last section treats the seventh day, the day of the Sabbath rest; cf. Bedjan, III.129-151. On the Syriac Hexaemeral tradition in general, see ten Napel, "Some Remarks on the Hexaemeral Literature in Syriac."

[5] The Greek tradition is much fuller; other relatively contemporary compositions include the *Commentary* of Eusebius of Emesa and the *Questions on Genesis* of Theodoret. In the Syriac tradition, the *Commentary* of Ephrem, and the *Homilies on Creation* of Narsai are essentially the only other such works; cf. bibliography below, for specific references.

[6] Both Jacob of Edessa (d. 708) and Anastasius of Sinai (d.c. 700) wrote extensive commentaries on the six days of creation.

[7] The text of Homilies 8 and 9 have survived in a Vth century manuscript; cf. Thomson, *Syriac Version of the Hexaemeron by Basil of Caesarea*, vol. 550, pp. v–vi. The work was apparently popular enough to require a second translation in the middle of the seventh century, though whether it was an entirely new translation or a revision of the first is unknown; cf. Barsoum, *Scattered Pearls*, 332.

(Syr., ܩܘܒܬܐ) ll. 552, 665, 791; roof (Syr., ܬܛܠܝܠܐ) l. 664; ceiling (Syr., ܬܛܠܠܐ) ll. 667, 794; vault (Syr., ܩܡܪܐ) l. 669; and dome (Syr., ܩܘܡܪܐ) l. 683.[8]

Unlike the light and the other elements that were created on day one, the firmament was not something created but was something made; that is, it was not made *ex nihilo* but was fashioned or composed from previous existing elements, in this case—most likely—from water (see note 11, below). It was positioned as a roof (or dome, etc.) above the earth but it served also as a dividing wall that maintained a permanent separation between the lower waters below and the upper waters above. Above this firmament God set that realm that is one entirely of light and in which there is no movement of time. It is also a realm that is completely without motion or movement and which has only rarely been even glimpsed. The realm below, on the other hand, is the realm where mankind lives and dwells and which is familiar to all; it is rather a realm of interchanging light and darkness, of days, months and seasons and other movements of time, not to mention varying climates characterized by such things as winds, storms, earthquakes, etc.

Beginning on this very second day, this just-named darkness first appeared. Unlike the first day when the darkness was produced by the presence of clouds, this newly formed firmament now became the cause for all subsequent darkness. According to Jacob, this was neither a bad thing nor a punishment, it rather provided the occasion for rest and reinvigoration for the work of the next day. This second day thus established a new pattern from the first day, and this new pattern then became the model for all subsequent days.

As he does throughout this entire long *Mêmrâ* 71, Jacob follows the biblical text fairly closely, that is, literally. Which is to say, that he tends to expostulate on what the text gives him, even if he seems to the modern mind to spin off into speculations not clearly

---

[8] Ephrem uses no such analogy in his *Commentary on Genesis*, while Jacob's contemporary and theological antagonist Narsai confines himself to a single analogy: ceiling (Syr., ܬܛܠܠܐ); cf. *Homélies de Narsaï sur la création*, I.55, II.296, III.145, 155. Curiously, neither employs the word found in the Peshitta of Psalm 104:2: curtain/tent (Syr., ܝܪܝܥܐ).

found in the text. But he does not, like some of his contemporaries, speculate here on such questions as why the creation of water and the creation of darkness received no mention at all here, or when the angels were created or how many heavens there are.

Summary

I. God is first a 'Creator', then a 'Maker' (521–548)

II. The Firmament divided the upper from the lower waters (549–604)

III. The Area above the Firmament is completely still and serene (605–632)

IV. Like the Firmament, Man is placed between the waters (633–660)

V. The Firmament is a roof over this world, the source of night (661–698)

VI. The Firmament was established for the benefit of mankind (699–794)

VII. The Firmament was created incomplete, without sun, stars and moon (795–822)

VIII. Day Two was the first moment in the planned progression of Creation (823–842)

Text and Translation

Homily 71b: On the Fashioning of Creation: The Second Day

I. God is first a 'Creator', then a 'Maker'

521 "And the Lord said, 'Let there be a firmament in the midst of the waters
and let it separate the waters [below] from the waters above.'"[1]
Day one arose and came forth without any progression
for it did not move until it went off to yield its place.
525 But the Lord appointed and ordained that day
and made it to be the measure and the model for its fellow days:
The east did not give it birth when it arose,
nor did the west give it burial when it set.
That Maker appointed and ordained it just as He willed;
530 He summoned and brought forth that second day that it too should "come to be."[2]
He made it the pattern for evening and dawn, and He established them
that they might always be opening and closing a great gate.
This [day] was a step down from that height of creation;
it was lower and existed on a different level – that of 'making'.

---

[1] Genesis 1:6, with the addition of "above" at the end, presumably to fulfill the requirements of the poetic line.

[2] The Syriac word ܢܗܘܐ used here is the first word in the Peshitta text of Genesis 1:6, just cited; "let there be", however, just does not fit the English grammatical construction here, hence the necessity here of the slightly altered translation "come to be".

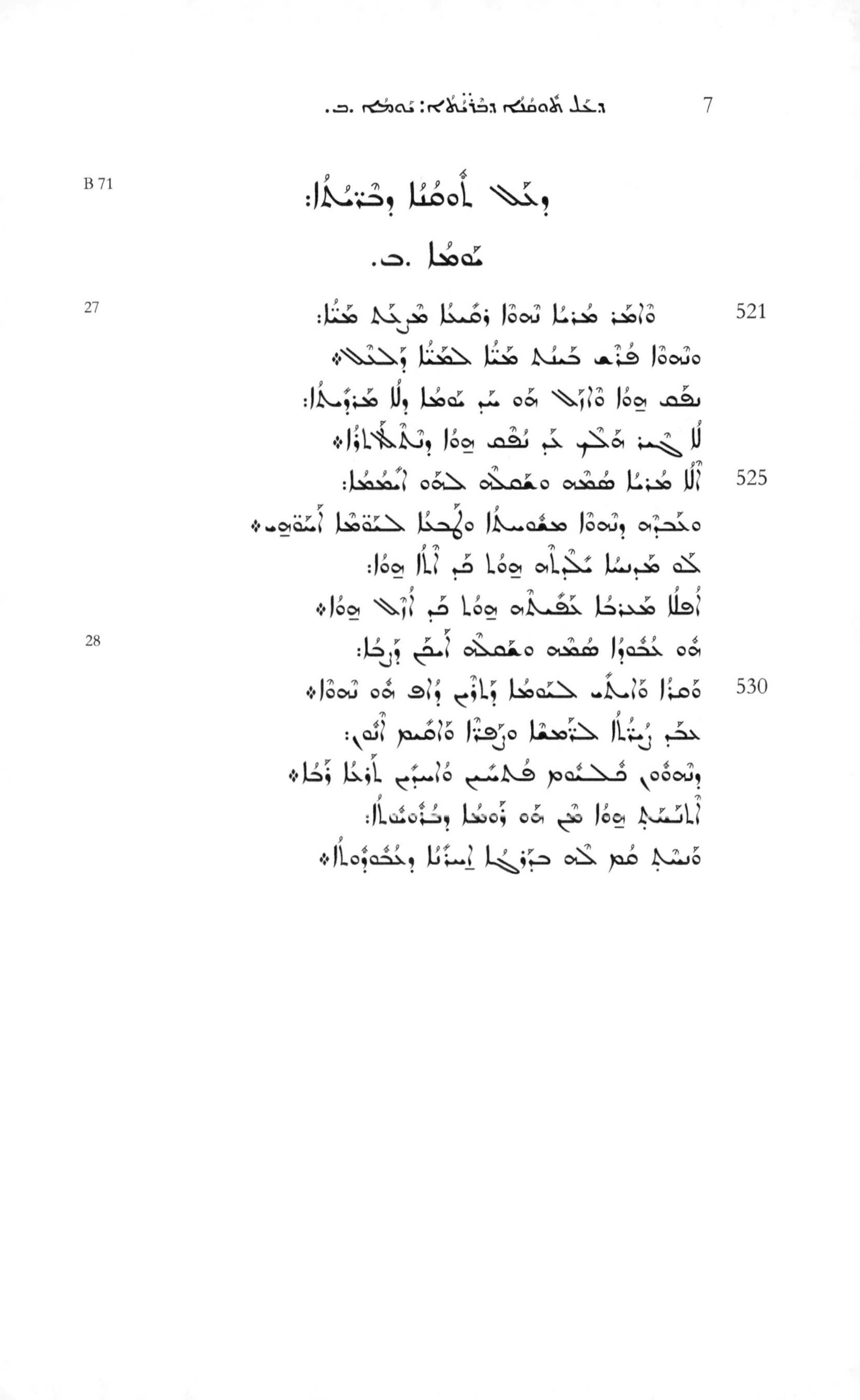

535 When creating the heavens and the earth He is 'Creator',
whereas when fashioning various created things He is 'Maker'.[3]
He created creation with a signal[4] and His hidden power established it,
and from that He began to make beautiful things in six days.
Before everything He was Self-Existent[5] with no need for created things
540 and His Existence[6] has no name except "He is."[7]
When He condescended and created things from nothing
He received the name 'Creator' because He created.
Then when He began to make those beautiful things that came to be
He consented to be called 'Maker' as well.
545 He is 'Maker' when He makes a thing from another thing,
but 'Creator' when He creates from nothing.

---

[3] Bou Mansour, *La théologie de Jacques de Saroug*, I, 33–45, discusses this distinction in Jacob's thought under the headings "*creatio ex nihilo*" and "*creatio continua*". The same distinction can also be found in his contemporary Narsai; see, for example, *Homélies de Narsaï sur la création*, II.325ff.

[4] As noted in many previous fascicules in this series, this 'signal' – or 'nod' – is a key concept in Jacob's notion how God created the world without working; see especially K. Alwan, "Le 'remzo' selon la pensée de Jacques de Saroug."

[5] Syr., *'îtyâ*.

[6] Syr., *'îtûtâ*.

[7] Syr., *'îtawhy*. This name, of course, derives from that which God revealed of His name to Moses at Exodus 3:14; the text of the Peshitta at Exodus 3:14 simply transliterates the Hebrew phrase which RSV translates "I am who I am". The words just translated "Self-Existence" and "Existence" both derive from the same root as the word translated here "He is"; for our translation see Mathews, *Jacob of Sarug's Homilies on the Six Days of Creation: The First Day*, 70, 89–134, and notes ad loc., especially n. 11.

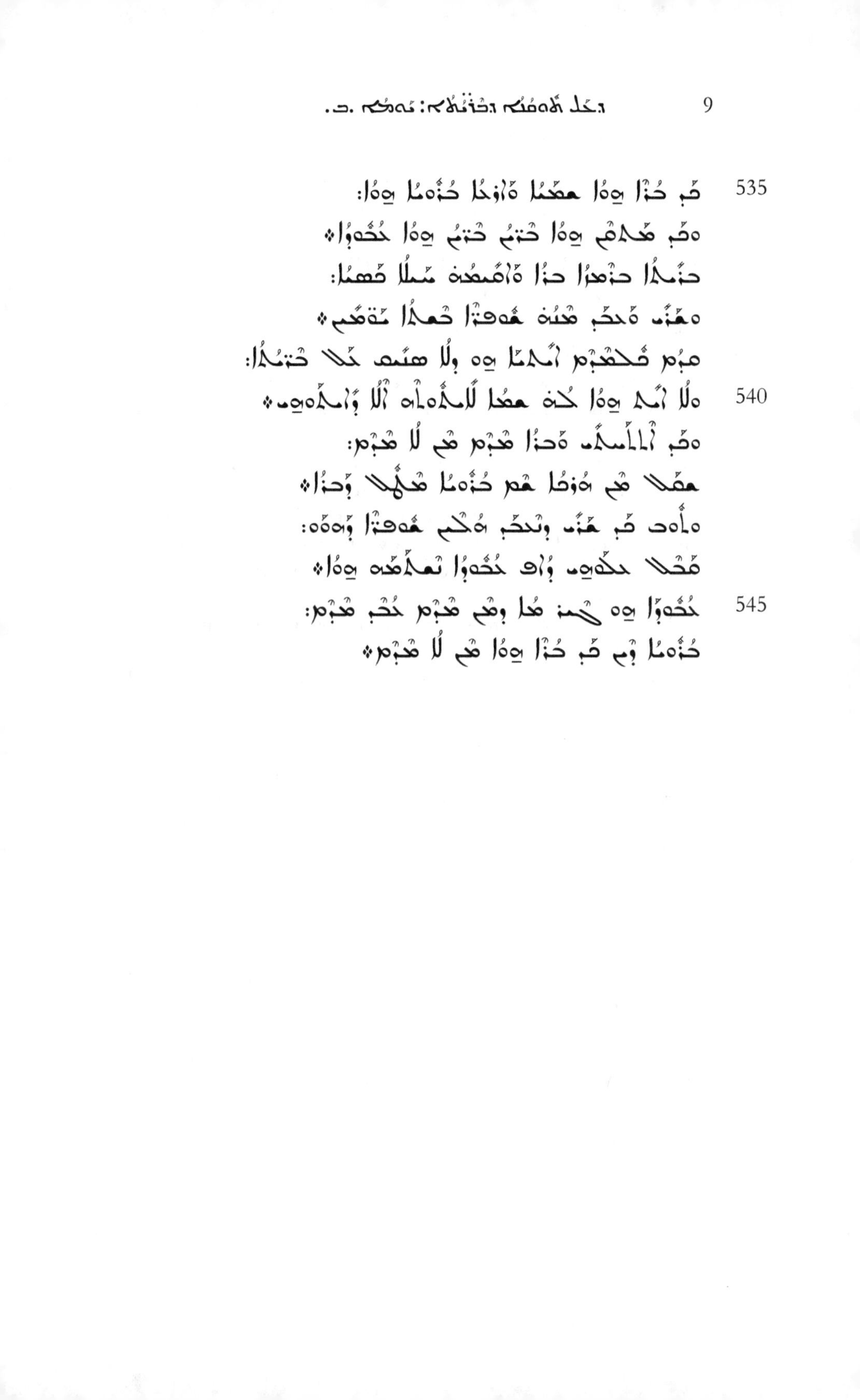

He created the earth unformed and desolate,[8]
but He began to form it and to build it up by 'making' it.[9]

II. THE FIRMAMENT DIVIDED THE UPPER FROM THE LOWER WATERS

God said, "Let there be a firmament between the waters;"[10]
550   this is something made, it was not a creation from nothing.[11]
From that thing which the signal of His creative activity established
He made the firmament on the second day as a tent for a dwelling place.
He commanded the wind that was hovering over the flood waters[12]
and it rose up between those waters in order to separate them.
555   At His command He divided them and put them in balance,
He also established them in their own places just as He willed.
He set the firmament in their midst as the boundary between the two sides
and He separated them so that each would stand within its own boundary.
He summoned the upper [waters] and raised them up to a high place,

---

[8] Genesis 1:2. Jacob's definitions here for "tohu and bohu" seem to be exceptional in Syriac literature; they are neither the definitions of his usual source Ephrem, *Commentary on Genesis*, I.3 ("void and desolation") nor of later Syriac tradition.

[9] Or, "by His making", or even "by His capacity to make"; Syr., ܥܒܘܕܘܬܗ to be distinguished from "His creative activity" or "His capacity to create" Syr., ܒܪܘܝܘܬܗ.

[10] Genesis 1:6.

[11] He nowhere makes it explicit, but Jacob presumably follows Ephrem in maintaining that the firmament was actually made from the waters (*Commentary on Genesis*, I.17), particularly since Narsai seems also to hold to the same teaching; cf. *Homélies de Narsaï sur la création*, I.51–52, II.297–298. III.142–143, and the discussions in T. Jansma, "Investigations into the Early Syrian Fathers on Genesis," 114–116, and idem., "L'Hexaméron de Jacques de Sarûg," 17, n.55, where he provides names of a number of others who also held this teaching.

[12] Genesis 1:2, and cf. note 20, below.

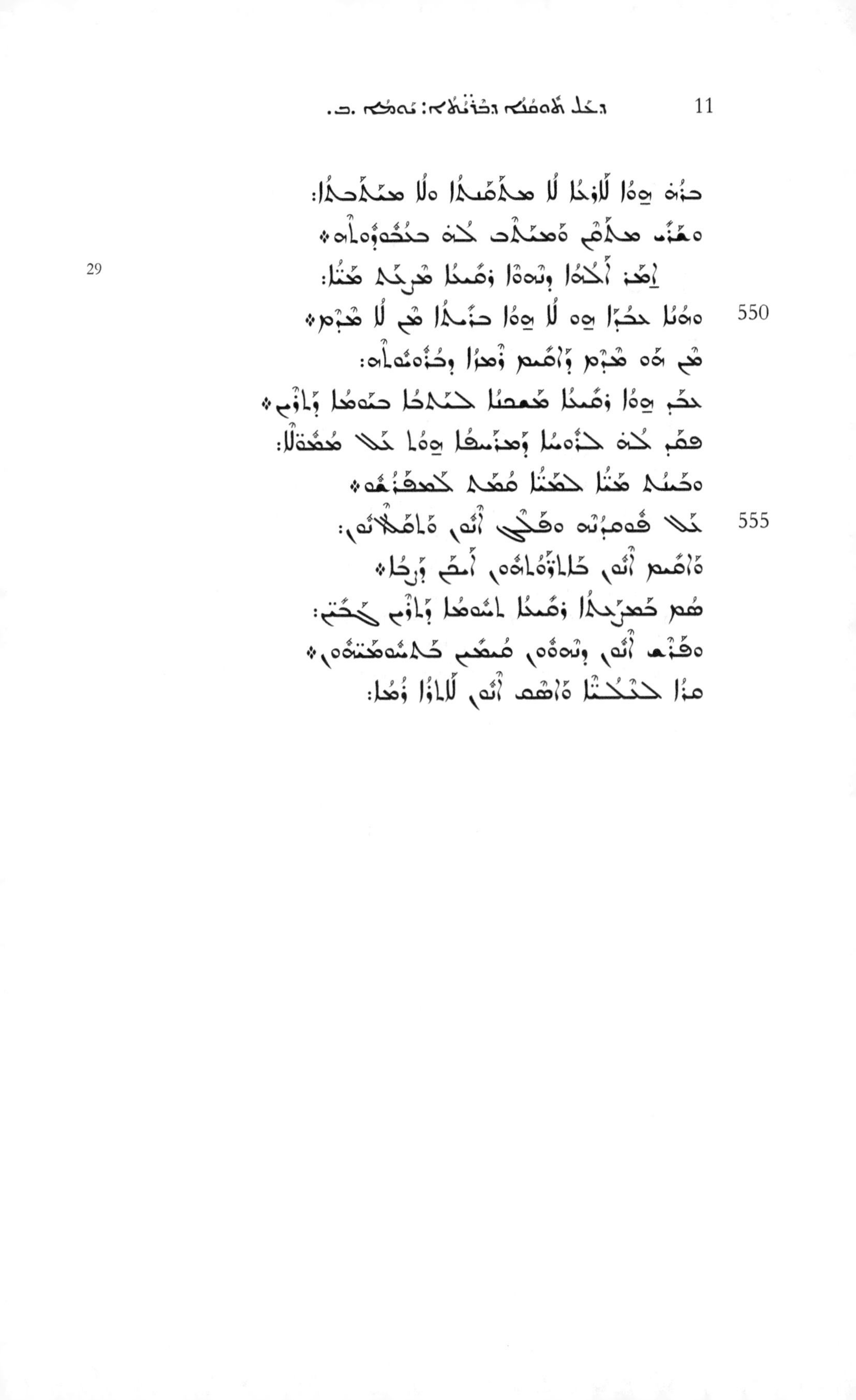

560   and they hastened there as if they were being poured into a lower place.
As if into a deep place the upper waters looked to ascend
into a high place speedily and with great haste.
As if through wadis they bore themselves off as they ascended,
that they might reach the place where the upper waters were sent.
565   They hastened to go up for the voice of the command impelled them;
although these [waters] were rising up it was like a cascade.[13]
They directed themselves to the height but as if they had found a deep cavity,
they were dragged there to go up and be still in that high place.
The apex of that high place was elevated like a cistern,
570   He drew them up and they remained there as if in a sea.
They did not abate as they rose up to that high place,
but they raced up there with great force as if into a chasm.
There they stood in that lofty dwelling above,
as if in a cavern surrounded by high mountains.
575   Behold, these waters were placid there upon that crest[14] of the firmament,
and did not flow down into the hollow place round about them.
As soon as He gave the command, "Let there be a firmament between the waters,"[15]
the upper waters hastened to a high place without delay.
Just as those lower [waters] gathered into a low place

---

[13] Or even, 'waterfall'; literally, "a descent". Our translation is clearly justified by the description of the force of the water's ascent[descent] as described by Jacob throughout this section.

[14] Syr., ܐܡܒܘܢ literally means "ambo, pulpit" (it is also the word for Gogoltha), but the underlying Greek word ἄμβων has an older definition of "rim", or "crest"; this older definition seems to better capture Jacob's meaning here.

[15] Genesis 1:6.

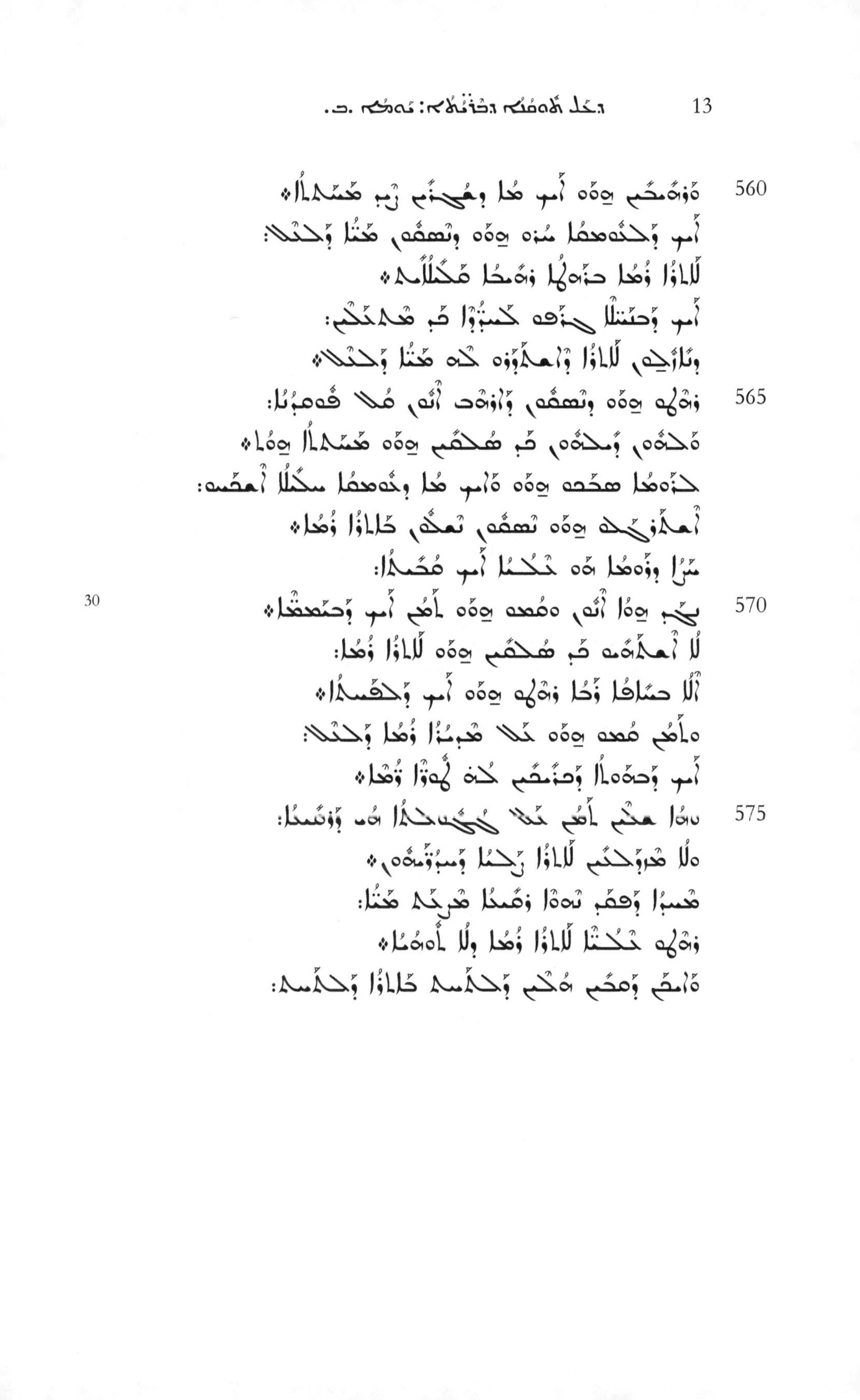

580	these too gathered into a high place without any effort.
	And just as the path to the upper heights was difficult for them,
	so too was the path difficult for the [lower waters] to descend to a hollow place.
	If someone were to go and bring the waters above down
	from their station, they would not slip down to the face of the deep.
585	Just as the lower waters run continuously downward,
	so too do the upper waters always remain firmly in the heights.
	Just as these waters were sent to their respective places by the Maker,
	they move quickly but there is nothing that can change the path He [laid out].[16]
	There is no way the upper [waters] can go down to the depth,
590	nor can the lower [waters] change the place in which they are confined.
	No nature can do anything of its own accord,
	unless it is commanded by the Creator.
	For it is easy for Him if He were to will to make fish fly
	or if He were to command birds to dive into the water.
595	A nature is something made, it has a Lord and He commands it,
	and there is never any way to oppose His command.
	It is not possible for fire to burn unless He were to command it,
	nor is it possible for water to be poured out unless He were to will it.
	There is a path in the sea and the hosts travel along it,
600	and wherever He wills He immerses companies in the sea.
	Dry land in the waters and rivers from flint![17]
	No nature can govern itself without [His] command.
	He established the deep as a nature and it exists just as He gave it that nature,
	and the Lord who established it can, however He wills, also destroy it.

---

[16] Literally, "His path".

[17] Jacob is alluding here to two of the great events of the Exodus: the crossing of the Red Sea, and the water that God brought forth from the rock in Rephidim; cf. Exodus 14:21 and 17:6, respectively.

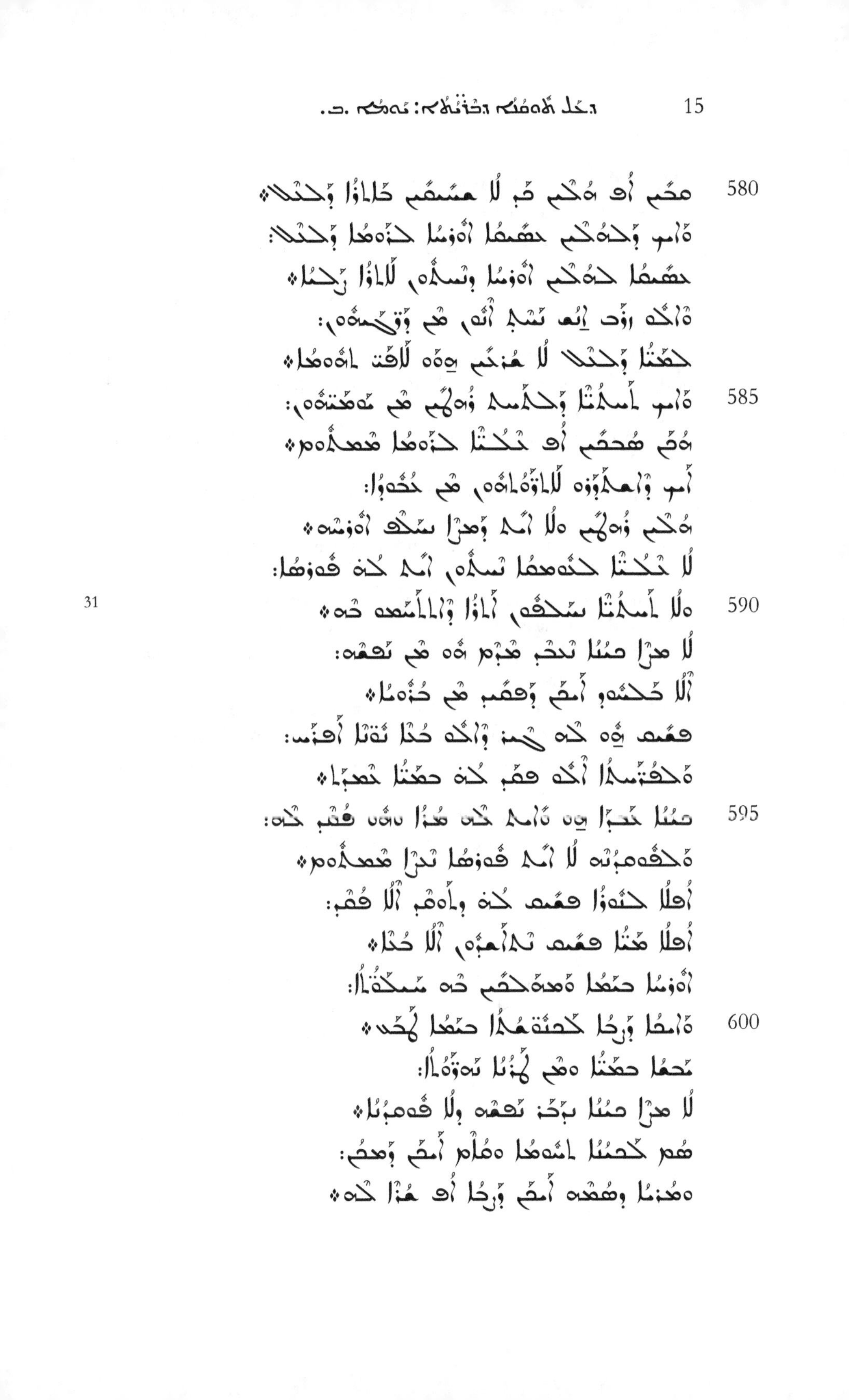

III. The Area above the Firmament is completely still and serene

605 On the second day [God] said, "Let there be a firmament in the waters;"[18]
He laid down a command, divided the waters and set their boundaries.
For the lower [waters] He set off a place in which they might stand,
and for the upper [waters] He fashioned a spot in which they might be confined.
The firmament was set in the midst and is established between the two sides;
610 according to His command, the waters remained still within their boundaries.
The wind, about which it is written "it was hovering over the flood waters,"[19]
was not hovering over where the upper waters were standing.
The wind that "was hovering" stood between the waters;
it remained below while the upper [waters] remained above without any "hovering".
615 For this reason, neither fish nor creeping things were produced
by the waters above for there was no wind blowing there.[20]
For the[se waters] were neither stirring nor moving, nor were they were producing,
for they were not placed there to produce but to remain still.
For no wind was blowing in those seas above,

---

[18] Genesis 1:6.

[19] Genesis 1:2.

[20] Jacob expands slightly on the teaching of Ephrem here. Jacob follows Ephrem who insists that this is a natural wind and not the Holy Spirit, arguing that the proof is in the fact that nothing new was produced in the waters (*Commentary on Genesis*, I.7); cf. discussion in T. Jansma, "Investigations into the Early Syrian Fathers on Genesis," 104–106, and for Ephrem, T. Kronholm, *Motifs from Genesis 1–11*, 43–44. Jacob here further clarifies by saying that above the firmament it is not even an issue as in that upper realm there is to be found no wind, not even any movement or motion of any sort.

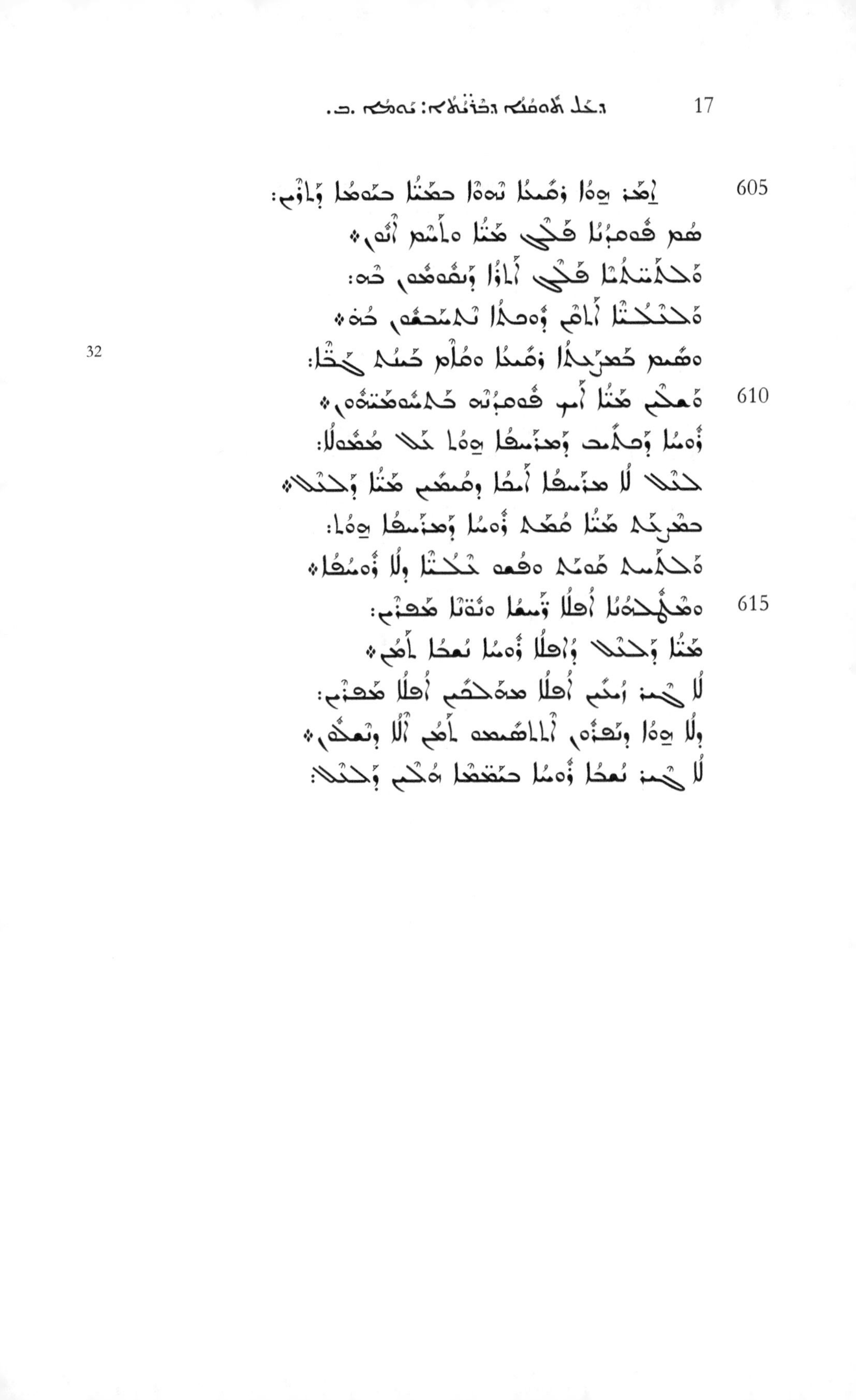

620 nor does any ministering wind ever enter that place there.
There are no clouds moving in that tranquil place,
nor do thunder or lightning arise within its confines.
There are there no winds, no breezes, no storms,
nor any disturbance as there are in the lower waters.
625 They are still and calm and they remain there serene,
there is no movement, breeze or wind there.
The light is hidden and the waters are confined in that tranquil place,
their color is so beautiful that even the sun is not as beautiful.
Along their lower side is the firmament, a solid body
630 and below it are movements, breezes and a place in commotion.
Along their upper side is a magnificent light and a great peace,
and the places of the hosts are within their boundaries.

IV. LIKE THE FIRMAMENT, MAN IS PLACED BETWEEN THE WATERS

Direct your mind here, O you who want to learn, if you are discerning;
be amazed and wonder, look and marvel at where you were placed.
635 In the midst of the waters, between the upper and the lower,
above you and below you, the waters were placed.
The abyss is below you, while the flood waters are above you;
while they are collected and stand there, you are in their midst but do not marvel!
Between the seas you are confined, you of little consequence,
640 in the place that is between those waters that have been separated.
Behold, the upper [waters] are above your head in a high place,
and lo, the lower are beneath your feet, a great abyss.
Both the upper and the lower [waters] are bound to the signal,
lest they breach and overwhelm you, you of little significance.

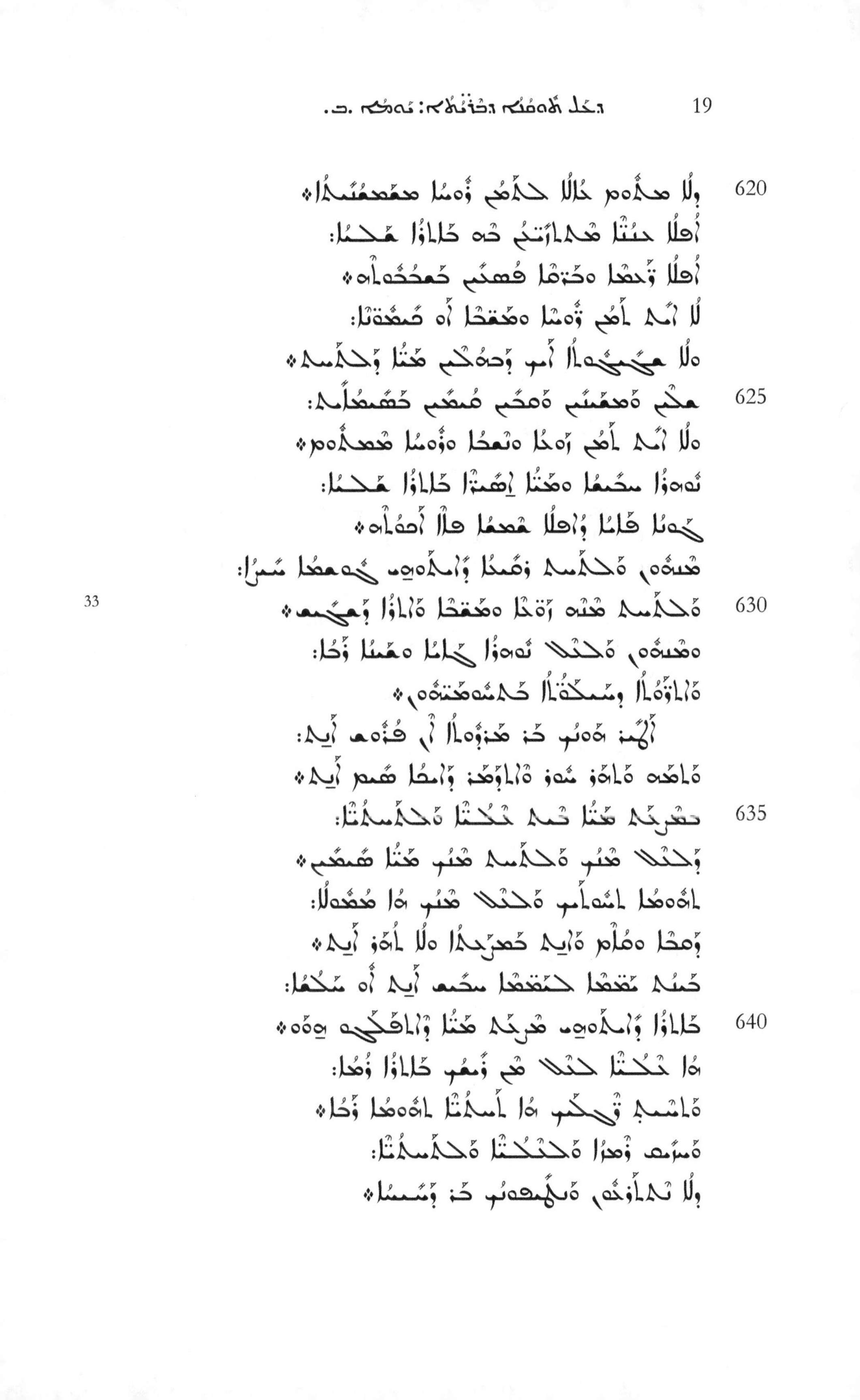

645 If you were to notice how small and trivial your place is,
 you would swoon at how numerous are your perils.
 If you would consider how you are preserved between these dangers,
 you would be unable to keep yourself from giving praise.
 Lift up your eyes and see who it is who created you,
650 which even this scripture demands from the discerning.
 Know where you are and consider that place where you have been set,
 and in wonder render thanksgiving for His ability to make.[21]
 Between the seas He enclosed you when He created you,
 like something wild so that you not become rebellious.
655 Yet you fret, you stir up trouble, and you cause dispute;
 you are puffed up, haughty and put yourself on a pedestal.
 You are a lump of clay and were placed in the flood waters of the sea;
 Look upon yourself, marvel and give thanks to the Godhead
 who bent down the heights, stretched out the depths and gathered the seas,
660 and directed His signal to these places and their boundaries.

V. The Firmament is a roof over this world, the source of night

The firmament stood between the waters on the second day,
 just as the Lord had commanded by the signal of His ability to make.[22]
 There is a boundary between the [lower] and the upper waters,
 and it serves as a roof for this enclosed place below.
665 It is a tent for that troubled dwelling of the whole world,
 and in its shade all creation has its beginning and its end.
 It is a ceiling for the great house of mankind
 which the signal of the Godhead built from nothing.
 It is like a suspended vault that stands with no foundations,

---

[21] See note 9, above.
[22] See note 9, above.

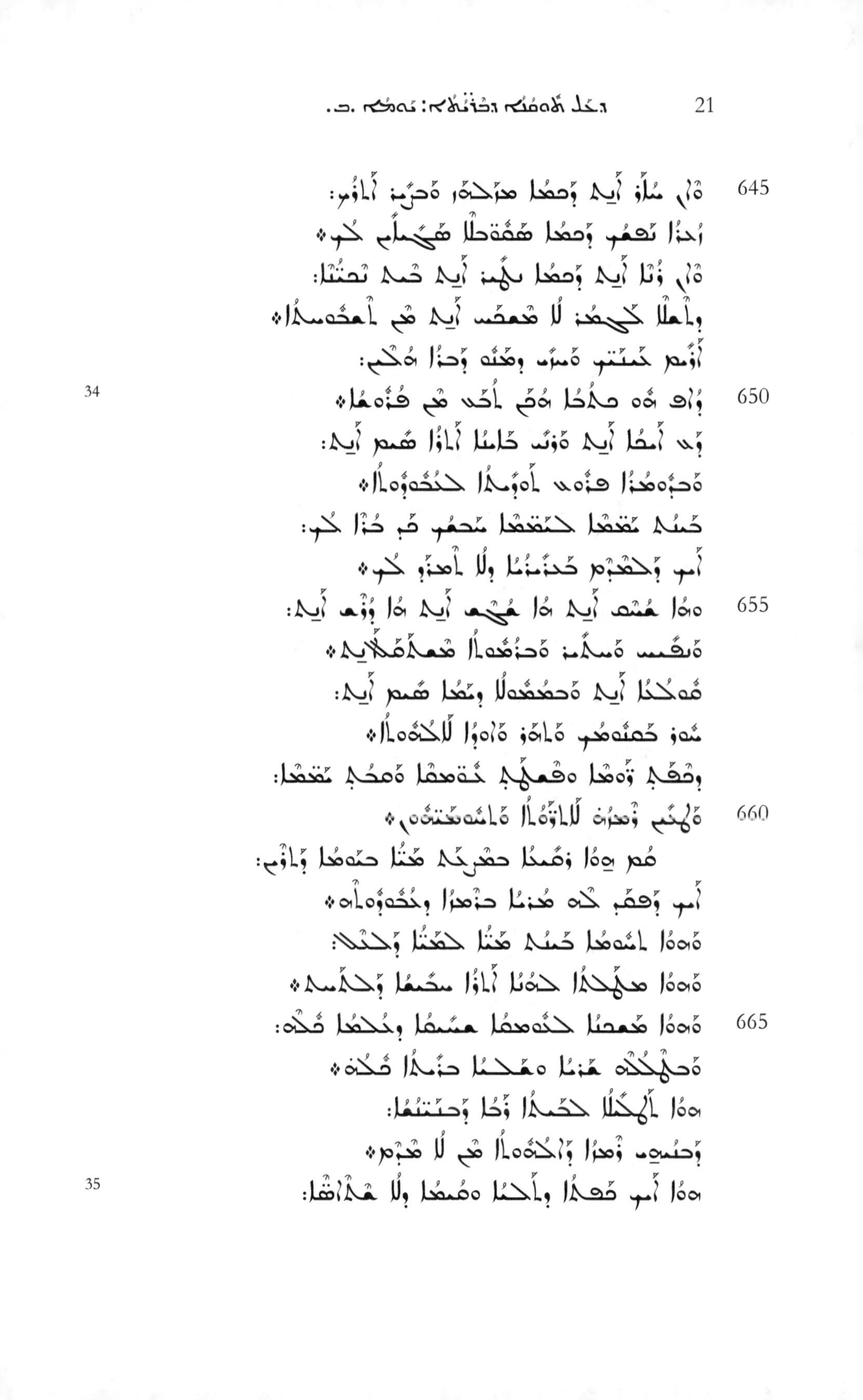

670	nor are there any pillars holding it up other than [His] signal.
	The firmament came into existence to bring night to the earth,
	for its shadow is the night and this is obvious.
	That first night came to be from a shadow,
	namely, that of the clouds by which the depths were hidden.[23]
675	For there was no firmament on that first day
	from which any darkness might rise or settle over creation.
	For the darkness on that first night arose from the clouds
	before the firmament even came into existence.
	On this second night that subsequently came to be,
680	the shadow came to be from this firmament which you can see.
	It shaded the house, there were no openings to the height above,
	and by its cover night settled over its inhabitants.
	It was set like a dome and above it is a great light,
	the pure waters and the places of the heavenly beings.
685	Above it there is neither night[24] nor shadow,
	whereas this place below has no lack of darkness.
	There are no lights that at one time rise and at another set,
	only the light of a single day that never changes.
	In that place there are no evenings, no mornings, no seasons,
690	nor are there days, nights or any passage of time.[25]
	A great light was gathered into that place like the flood waters,
	as Paul,[26] Ezekiel[27] and Stephen[28] all bear witness.[29]
	Every one who has attained a vision of the heavens opened,
	saw there a great light with great intensity.

---

[23] Ephrem, *Commentary on Genesis*, I.4, also posits the creation of these clouds that produced the darkness on the first day.

[24] The text here reads ܐܬܪܐ 'place', but I have chosen the alternate reading, ܠܠܝܐ 'night' which seems to make better sense here.

[25] Literally, "swift course [of time]".

[26] Cf. Acts 9:3; this citation alone of the following three explicitly mentions light. Cf. also Acts 22:6, 26:13.

[27] Cf. Ezekiel 1:26–28.

[28] Cf. Acts 7:55–56.

[29] Ephrem, *Commentary on Genesis*, I.4, cites these same three biblical figures as witnesses of the light above the firmament.

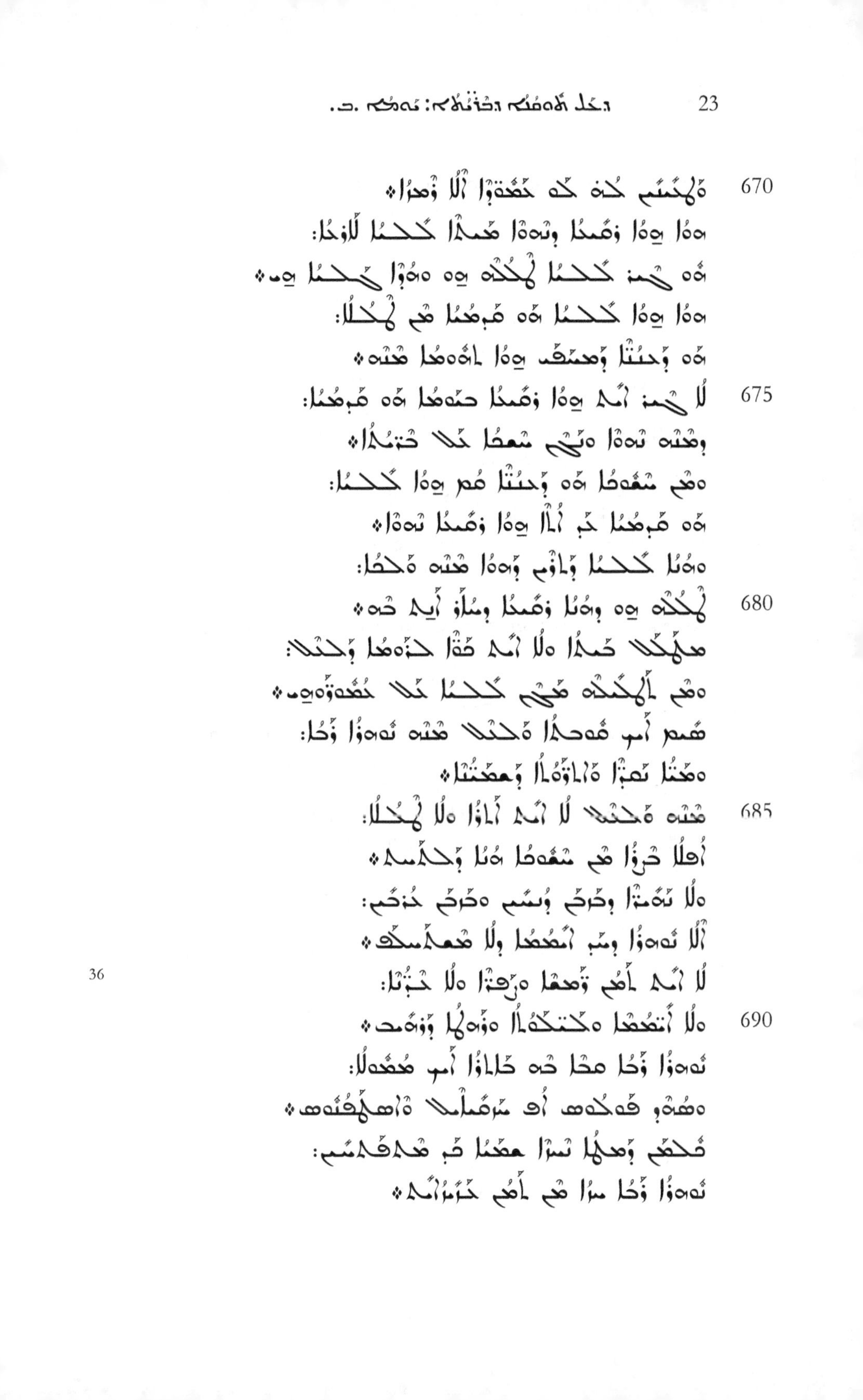

695 Because no openings are permitted into that place, our place is dark
and we live half of our life in the night.
If that Maker had not put this borrowed light in our place,
then our place would have been entirely dark.

VI. THE FIRMAMENT WAS ESTABLISHED FOR THE BENEFIT OF MANKIND

The great light concealed from us the firmament that came to be;
700 lo, our place is enclosed and nights take their turns[30] within it.
The firmament that came to be on the second day, as we said,
produced the night by its shadow over creation.
The Maker also established it for the sake of the world,
that below it there might be a house for all sorts of things,
705 that both nights and days might occur within it,
as well as months, weeks, years and other revolving periods of time,
so that in the day the activity of humankind might take place,
and at night there be rest for those who work and toil.
There was in it a light that hastens everything to its task,
710 as well as a darkness to be a set time for the greedy to cease.
[God] perfectly constructed the course of the night and of the day
in this house that is full of tedium for those that are in it.
For if there had been no night for the industrious
who would do the tedious chores or the tiresome work?
715 And if there were no evening to admonish the greedy to cease,
it would kill their companions in their overexertion.
That one who is concerned for His creatures would arrange them,
measure the times and put in place aids for all that they do.
He provided a world for one to be active at times and idle at other times,

---

[30] Reading ܡܫܚܠܦ "change, take turn", instead of ܡܫܬܥܐ "play, sport; narrate, tell" with Bedjan, p. 36, n. 3; the confusion of ܠ and ܬ in Syriac manuscripts is a fairly common one.

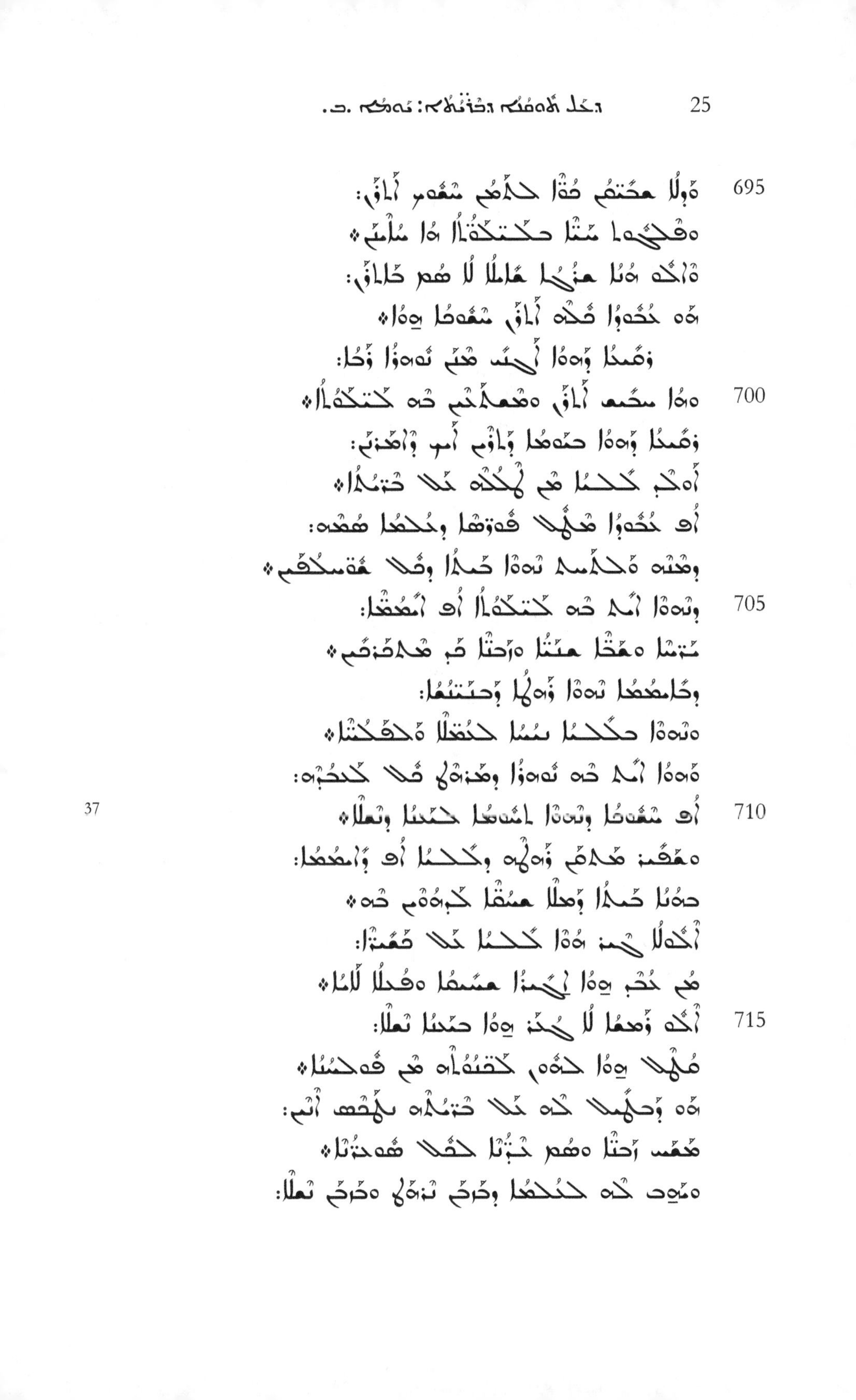

720	to be wearied at times and to rest from labor at other times.
	With measures, numbers, and with calculations,
	let all the affairs of mankind continue.
	There is a beginning and there is an end to their actions,
	a morning for girding oneself, an evening for unwinding and a night to sleep,
725	summer for being active and winter to cease from one's labor,
	and of everything may its proper time be known.
	For this reason the Maker established evenings and mornings
	with their limits that they might occur at their proper times.
	He commanded and this firmament came to be on the second day,
730	that by its cover there might be night just as you have heard,
	and that it may stand between the waters [below] and the waters above,
	and that by it mankind's sight might be limited and not wander all over it.
	It is stretched out like a garment beneath the habitation of the Godhead,
	and like a ceiling above the dwelling-place of mankind.
735	The firmament is by name the sky but it is a firmament,
	for who is capable of [describing] those heavens above?
	Apart from Moses and the great Paul who spoke of them,
	who is as able to speak of them as they are?
	Moses said, "The Lord created the heavens and the earth,"[31]
740	and a day later, "Let there be a firmament"[32] was said.
	The firmament came to be and the heavens above were hidden by it,
	for the human eye is unable to endure them,
	due to their brightness, their glories and their beauties,
	and to that great sea of light that is without limit.

---

[31] Genesis 1:1.
[32] Genesis 1:6.

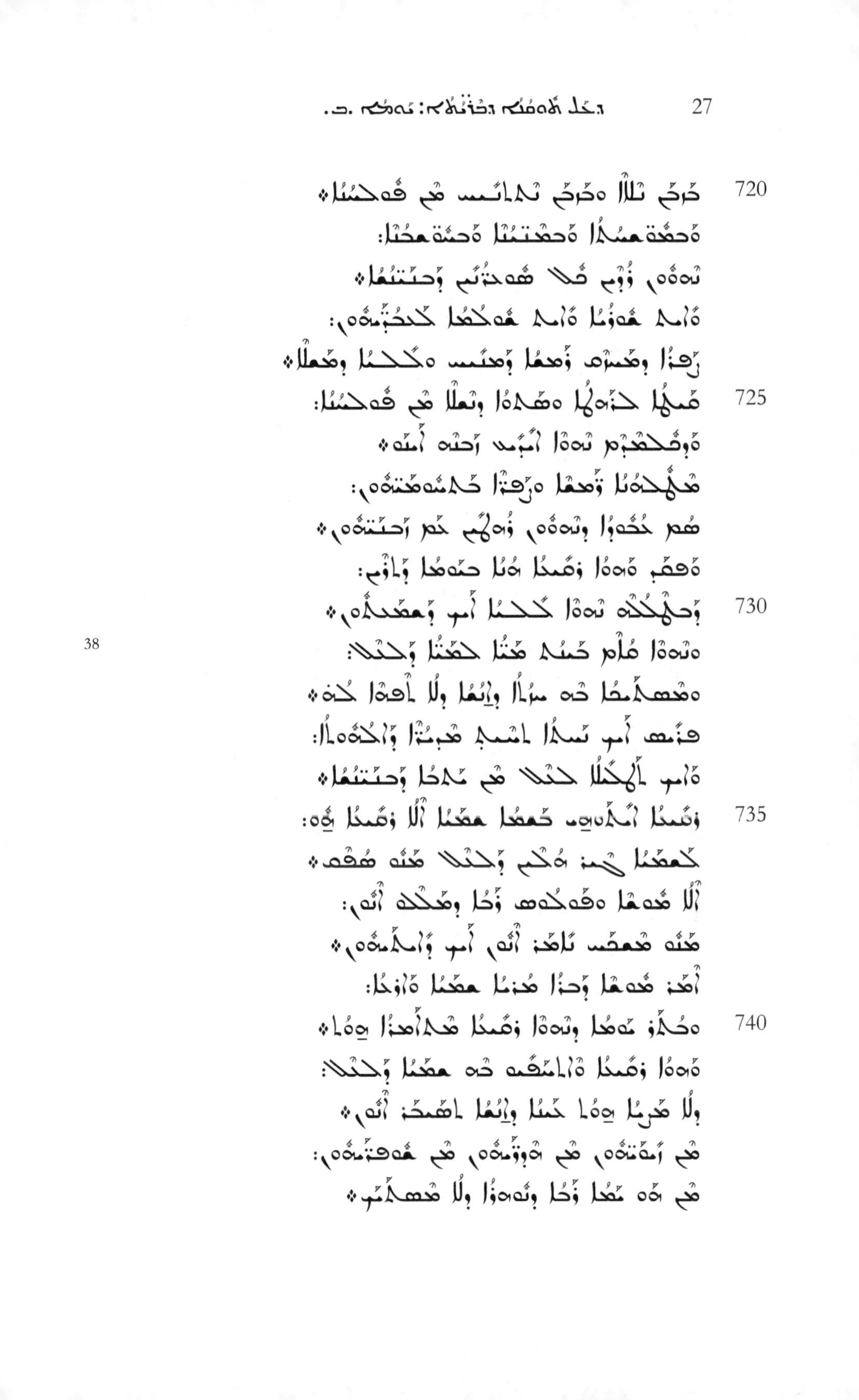

745	There is no sun in the heavens above for it is completely sun,
	and its light is gathered up at that gate of the firmament.
	Whenever it does go out from that light to our place,
	it excites, rouses and makes the one who saw it marvel.
	At one time Paul,[33] and before that Ezekiel,[34]
750	were witnesses of that light that the heavens above possess.
	And at the first signal it stood in a high place,
	and the firmament came to be on the second day that [this light] be hidden by it,
	so that the firmament might also be the sky for mankind,
	and the heavens for the house – for this house which is full of people.
755	The heavens above are honored by [the light]'s being concealed there,
	and no one sees it except the perfect and the divine.
	The firmament is a body and therefore there is also a shadow with it,
	whereas in those heavens above there is no body.
	But [the firmament] is a great thing that stands there spiritually,
760	for it is full of light and there it never turns to night.
	There is no shadow in those heavens above,
	from which shadow there would be a night on that day.
	In the place of the shadow lights pour forth; thus, they call
	those who dwell there in that place above 'children of light'.
765	And this firmament that the Lord made on the second day
	is like a land below them for those above.
	It is the sky[35] for us and a land for those above it,
	for the signal shaped it to be a land for those above it.
	For us, the Creator made material vessels as bodies,

---

[33] Cf. Acts 9:3, 22:6, 26:13; and see note 26, above.
[34] Cf. Ezekiel 1:26–28.
[35] Or, 'heaven'.

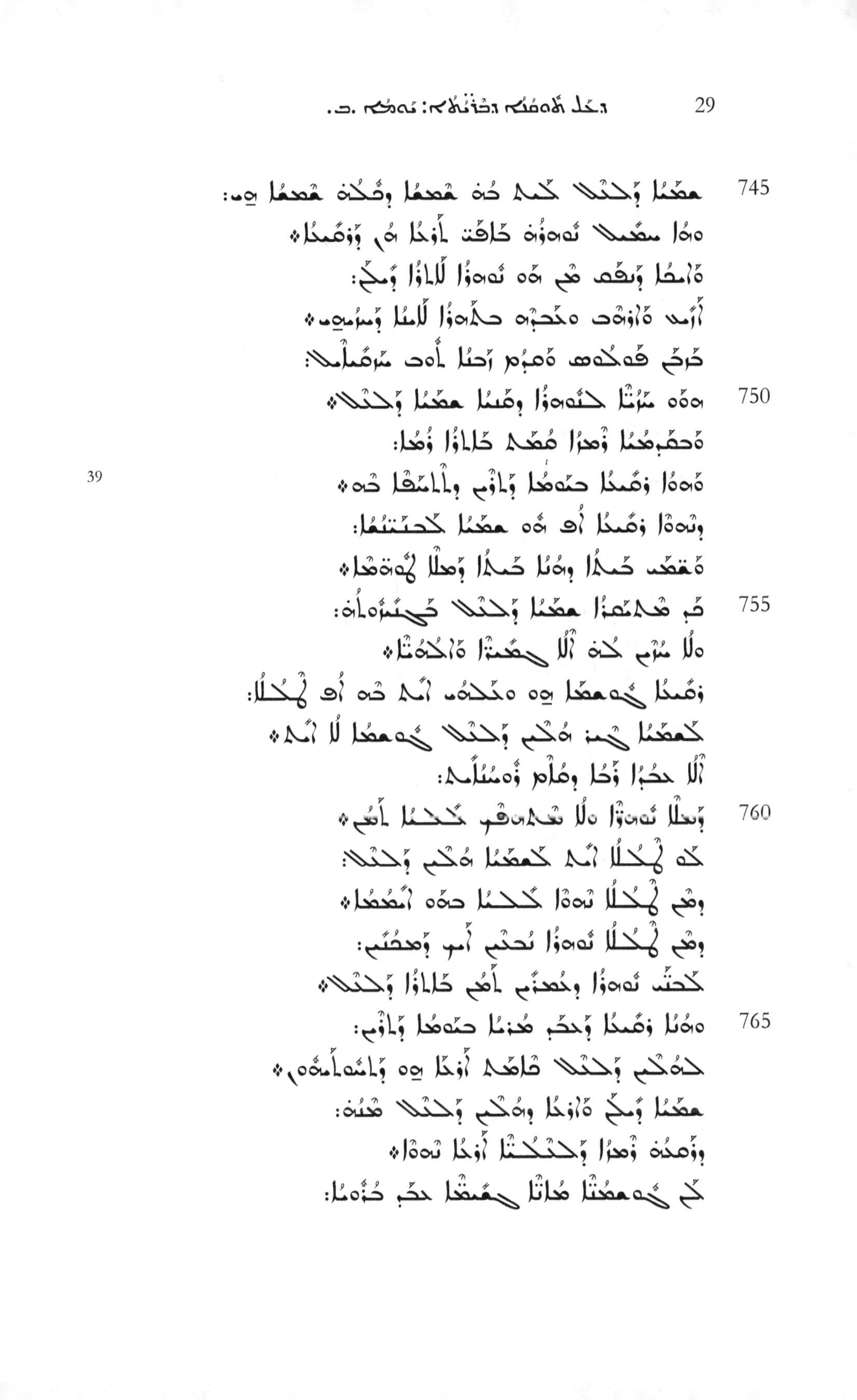

770 while for spiritual beings whatever is made there is spiritual.
The firmament is a sky for us for it has a body,
and makes night for us below by its shadow.
For us corporeal beings it is fitting that this thing be corporeal,
while for those who are incorporeal everything be spiritual.
775 For this reason when the heavens above were created,
its construction existed spiritually along with spiritual beings.
And the hosts by the spirit of the mouth of the Godhead
exist there spiritually within their boundaries.
In that place there is no dense body nor shadow,
780 nor such a night that exists here in our place.
All this creation is [made up] of bodies and of shadows;
like a sphere it is set entirely within nothing.
There is no body – not above it, not below it,
nor within its confines – except that power which supports it.
785 It is suspended and stands there like a bird within nothing,
and in its midst is a disorderly world full of motion.
Above this wheel which is supported on bodies
is a desert of light in which the hosts dwell.
And beneath them this firmament is like a sphere
790 in which are concealed those corporeal bodies.
It is fixed like a tent for the habitation of families and nations,
and in it dwell various sorts of things in their natures.
And the wisdom of the Most High spread it out on the second day,
like a ceiling for the entire world of mankind.

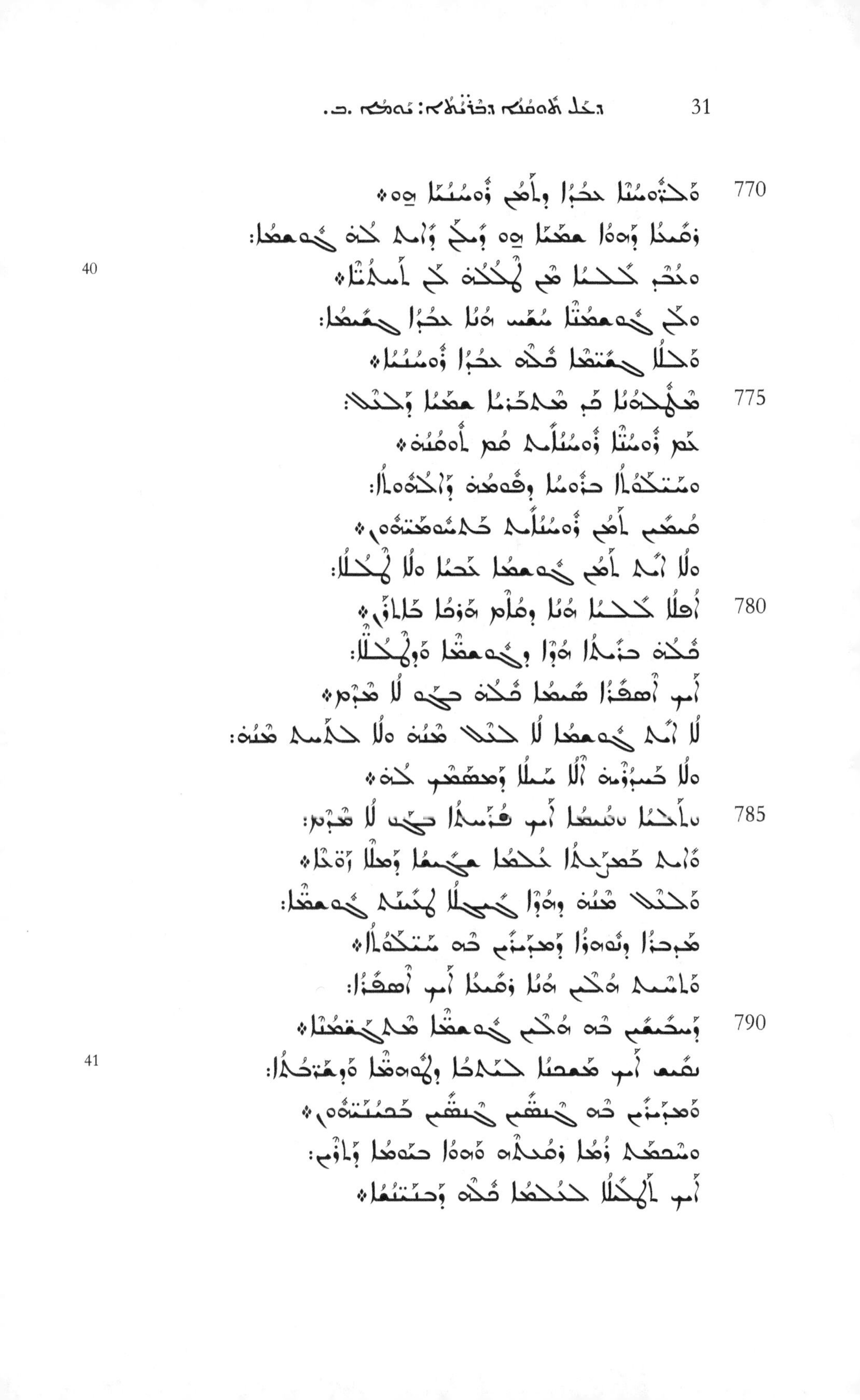

VII. The Firmament was created incomplete, without sun, stars and moon

795 He created the firmament without the lights arrayed upon it,
and without a sun or a moon that circulate on it.
He wove a great garment and He spread it out with no embroidery,
until He formed it and then painted it with His skillfulness.
And because it was lacking those lights [soon] to be arrayed upon it;
800 it is not written "The Lord saw that it was good" when He made it.
Whoever is attentive understands this teaching
in all the passages of prophecy and in their words.
On every [other] day it is written "The Lord saw that it was good,"[36]
but on this second day it is not said.
805 The firmament had come to be, but because it [still] required embroidery
the phrase "The Lord saw that it was good" was left out and was not written.[37]
Although He was soon to adorn it with ornaments and with lights,
He kept this for when it was finished; then it would be said.
For it was evident that He made no error when He created it,

---

[36] Genesis 1:12, 19, 21, 25 and 31.

[37] Again, Jacob follows Ephrem, *Commentary on Genesis*, I.20, on this explanation for the lack of the phrase in the Peshitta text (which follows here the Hebrew text). While one finds this same explanation in contemporary Jewish literature as well, the more predominant explanation there is that the reason that Moses did not call this day good was because hell had also been created on the second day; cf. L. Ginzberg, *Legends of the Jews*, I.15, and the accompanying note 54 in V.18–19. This phrase does occur, however, in the majority of Greek biblical texts, so see discussion of it in, for example, Basil, *Hexaemeron*, III.10; Theodoret, *Questions on Genesis*, X. The phrase is found in the early Armenian bible as well; see Eghishe, *Commentary on Genesis*, p. 22–25, though without comment or explanation. Narsai, however, no doubt due to his acquaintance with Theodore Mopsuestia and other Greek commentators, seems to have had this phrase in his text; cf. *Homélies de Narsaï sur la création*, III.168.

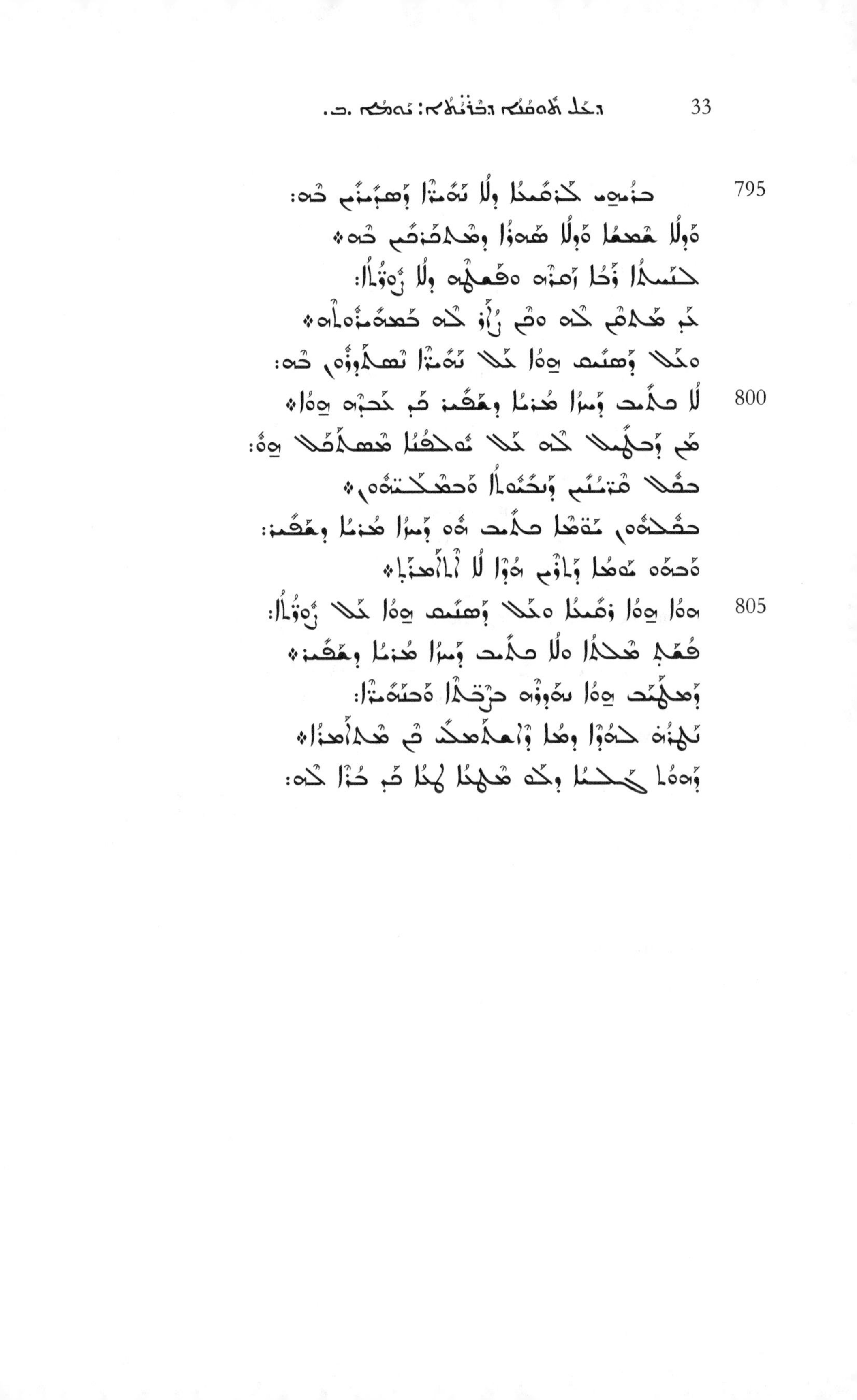

810   for He would soon create on it the sun, the moon and all the lights.
But because He is skillful and full of wisdom,
He delayed it so that its complete formation would exist in its time.
He did not wish to make the sun and the moon on the second day,
and if you are troubled you will learn this clearly enough.
815   He created the firmament between the waters and He divided them,
and He set the upper things and the lower things within their own boundaries.
Although it was not complete he made the firmament when He made it,
just as the earth was created without being formed.
Because another beauty was kept back to be added to it,
820   "He saw that it was good" was not said on the second day.
And the firmament was between the waters just as He had commanded:
"And there was evening and there was morning, a second day."[38]

VIII. Day Two was the First Moment in the Planned Progression of Creation

The world took hold of a path that it might come out from "tohu and bohu,"[39]
and the various periods began to proceed one after another.
825   Evenings and mornings proceeded to come forth within their own limits,
and He distinguished and took these times with their designations,
so evening took hold of the gate where night enters the world,
and morning, its brother, the gate that opens up onto the day.
And they stood and watched carefully over their posts,
830   they are not stolen nor do they steal one from the other.

---

[38] Genesis 1:8.

[39] Genesis 1:2; these "tohu and bohu" are the Hebrew words of this verse, which are transliterated – not translated – in the Peshitta version; they are translated "without form and void" in the RSV.

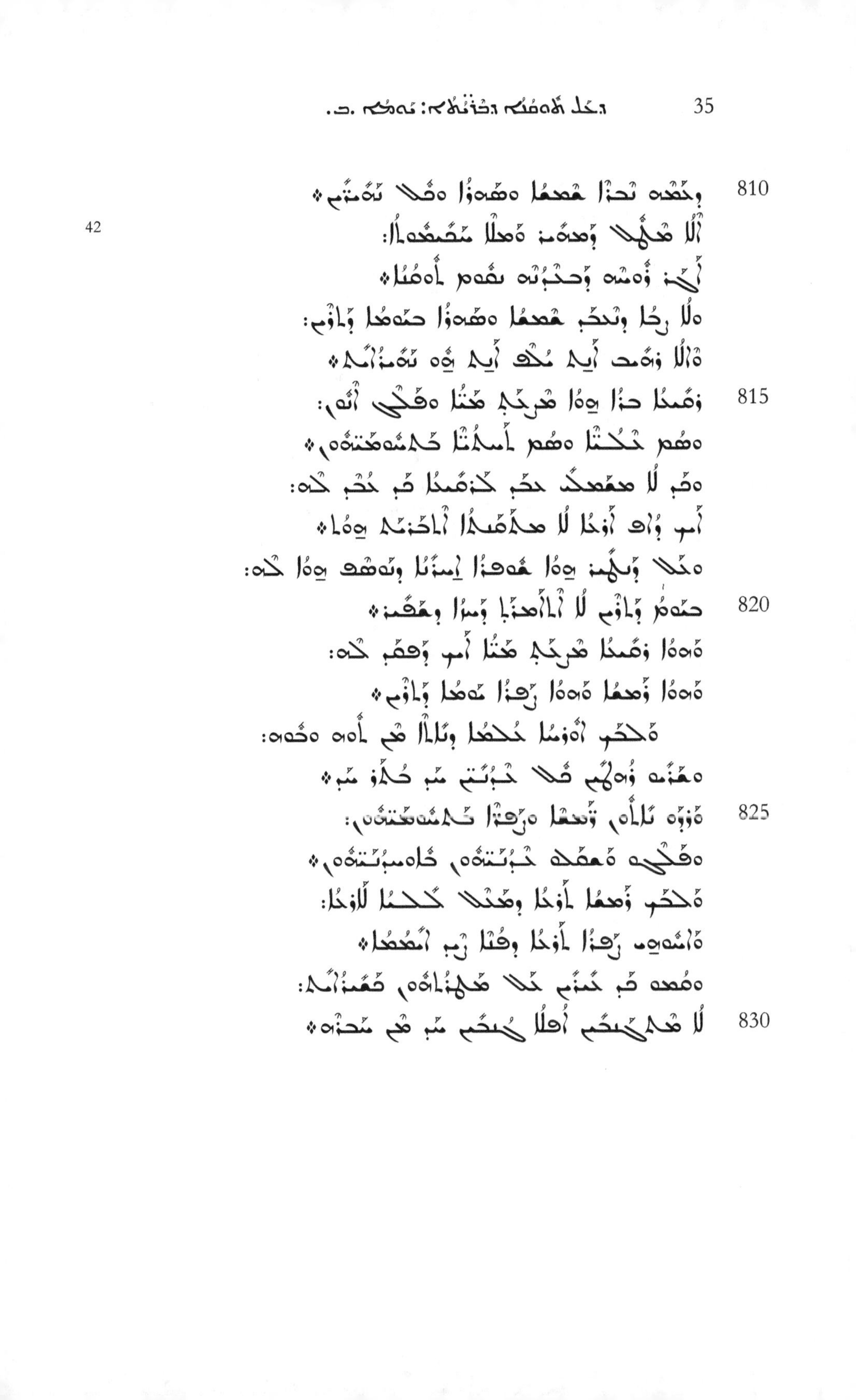

He measured and each one of them took hold of all its own hours,
that each might keep what is its and it not be apportioned to its counterpart.
Night was designed not to overstep the day,
nor day to draw near to the watch of night.
835 With justice and with proportion and with equality
they would continue and not be greedy toward one another.
Lo, they take hold of their path and come one after the other,
evenings and mornings according to the limits set down by the Creator.
The world proceeded, a first day and a second day,
840 and they began quickly to progress along their course.
The first [day] came and the second day followed in its footstep,
and then they gave way to the third that it too may come.

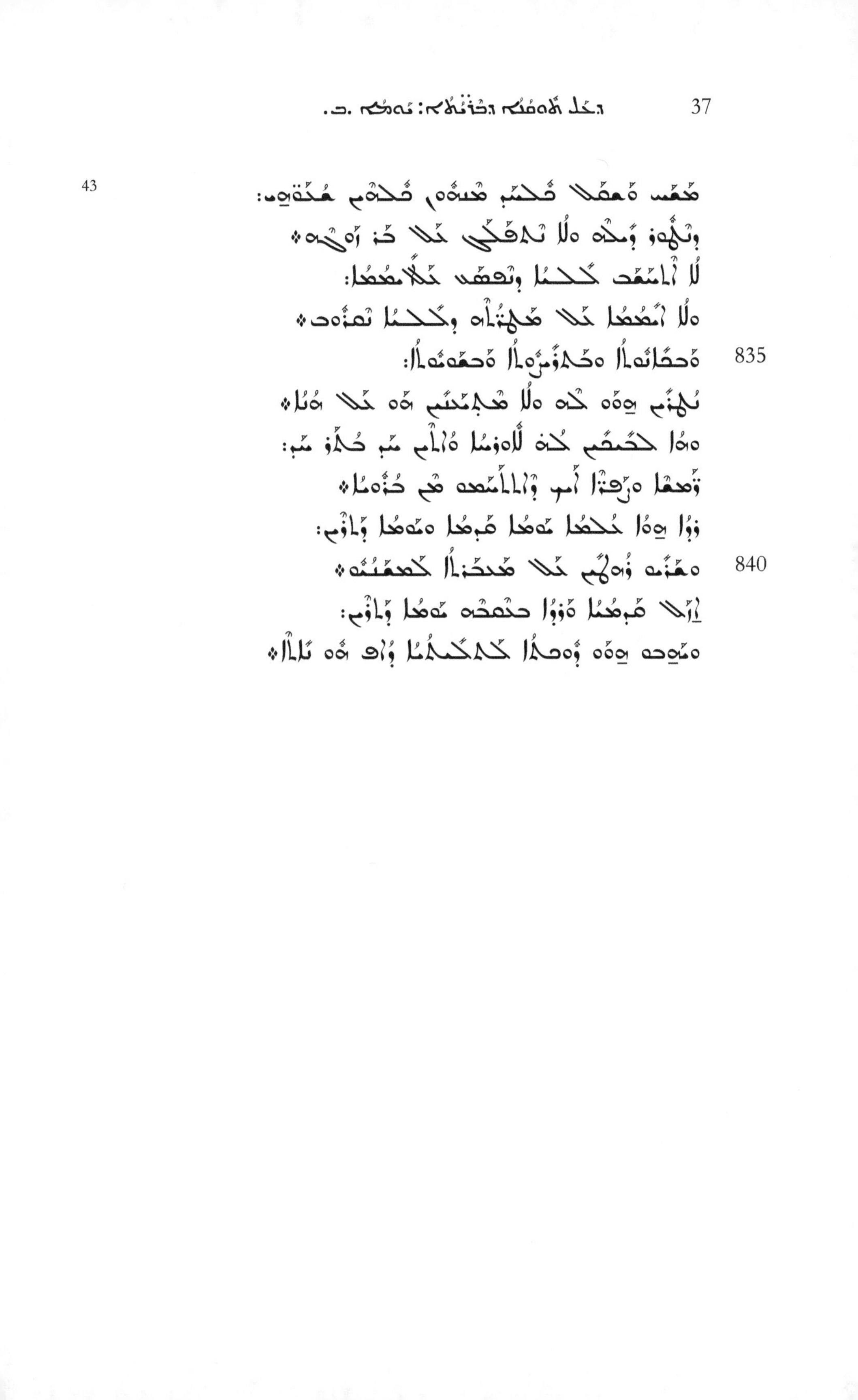

BIBLIOGRAPHY OF WORKS CITED

PRIMARY TEXTS

Eusebius of Emesa

Petit, Françoise, Lucas Van Rompay and Jos. J.S. Weitenberg, trs., *Eusèbe d'Émèse, Commentaire de la Genèse.* Traditio Exegetica Graeca, 15; Louvain: Peeters, 2011.

Basil

Giet, Stanislas, ed., *Saint Basile, Homélies sur l'Hexaméron.* Sources Chrétiennes, 26bis; Paris: Editions du Cerf, 1968. English translation in Blomfield Jackson, tr., *The Hexaemeron of Saint Basil.* A Select Library of Nicene and Post-Nicene Fathers. Second Series. Grand Rapids, 1976. Vol. 8, pp. 52–107.

Thomson, Robert W., ed. and tr., *The Syriac Version of the Hexaemeron by Basil of Caesarea.* CSCO 550–551; Louvain: Peeters, 1995.

Ephrem

Tonneau, Raymond M., ed. *Sancti Ephraem Syri in Genesim et in Exodum commentarii.* CSCO 152-53. Louvain: Peeters, 1955. English translation by Edward G. Mathews, Jr. in Edward G. Mathews, Jr. and Joseph P. Amar, *St. Ephrem the Syrian: Selected Prose Works.* Fathers of the Church, 91; Washington: Catholic University of America Press, 1994. Pp. 67–213.

Theodoret of Cyrus

Hill, Robert C., ed. and tr., *Theodoret of Cyrus, The Questions on the Octateuch. Volume 1: On Genesis and Exodus.* Library of Early

Christianity, 1; Washington: Catholic University Press, 2007.

Eghishe

Khachikyan, Levon, ed. and Michael Papazian, tr., *Commentary on Genesis by Eghishe*. Yerevan: Magaghat Publishing House, 2004.

Jacob of Sarug

Bedjan, Paulus, ed., with additional material by Sebastian P. Brock. *Homilies of Mar Jacob of Sarug*. 6 vols.; Piscataway: Gorgias Press, 2006 [original publication *Homiliae Selectae Mar-Jacobi Sarugensis*, 5 vols. Paris and Leipzig: Harrassowitz, 1905–1910].

Mathews, Jr., Edward G. *Jacob of Sarug's Homilies on the Six Days of Creation: The First Day*. Texts from Christian Late Antiquity, 27; Metrical Homilies of Mar Jacob of Sarug, 29. Piscataway: Gorgias Press, 2009.

Narsai

Gignoux, Philippe. *Homélies de Narsaï sur la création*. Patrologia Orientalis, 34.3–4 [161–162]. Turnhout: Brepols, 1968.

SECONDARY WORKS

Alwan, Khalil. "Le 'remzo' selon la pensée de Jacques de Saroug." *Parole de l'Orient* 15 (1988–1989), 91–106.

Barsoun, Ignatius Aphram I. *The Scattered Pearls: A History of Syriac Literature and Sciences*. Second Revised Edition. Piscataway: Gorgias Press, 2003.

Bou Mansour, Tanios. *La théologie de Jacques de Saroug. Tome I: Création, Anthropologie, Ecclésiologie et Sacraments*. Bibliothèque de l'Université Saint-Esprit, 36; Kaslik: l'Université Saint-Esprit, 1993.

Ginzberg, Louis. *The Legends of the Jews*. Volumes I, V. New York: Jewish Publication Society, 1909, 1913.

Jansma, Taeke. "Investigations into the Early Syrian Fathers on Genesis." *Oudtestamentische Studiën* 12 (1958), 69–181.

Jansma, Taeke. "L'Hexaméron de Jacques de Sarug." *L'Orient Syrien* 4 (1959), 3–42, 129–162, 253–284.

Jansma, Taeke. "Une homélie anonyme sur la création du monde." *L'Orient Syrien* 5 (1960), 385–400.

Kronholm, Tryggve. *Motifs from Genesis 1–11 in the Genuine Hymns of Ephrem the Syrian with particular reference to the influence of Jewish exegetical tradition.* Coniectanea Biblica. Old Testament Series, 11. Uppsala: Almqvist & Wiksell, 1978.

ten Napel, Erik. "Some Remarks on the Hexaemeral Literature in Syriac." In Hans J.W. Drijvers, Rene Lavenant, Collie Molenberg and Gerrart J. Reinink, eds., *IV Symposium Syriacum: Literary Genres in Syriac Literature.* Orientalia Christiana Analecta, 229. Rome: Pontificium Institutum Studiorum Orientalium, 1987. Pp. 57–69.

Index of Names and Themes

abyss (see also 'deep') 637, 642
Being 539
boundary (see also 'limit') 557, 558, 606, 610, 632, 660, 663, 778, 816
ceiling 667, 794
cloud 621, 674, 677
command 555, 565, 577, 594, 596, 597, 602, 606, 610
creation 533, 537, 550, 666, 676, 702, 781
Creator 535, 542, 546, 592, 769, 838
dark 695, 698
darkness 676, 677, 686, 710
dawn 531
day 523, 525, 526, 538, 688, 690, 705, 711, 762, 833, 834
 second day 530, 552, 605, 661, [679], 701, 729, 752, 765, 793, 804, 813, 820, 832, 839, 841
deep (see also 'abyss') 584, 589, 603, 674
dome 683
earth 535, 671
Essence 540
evening 531, 689, 715, 724, 822, 825, 827, 838
Ezekiel 692, 749
firmament 521, 549, 552, 575, 577, 605, 609, 629, 661, 671, 675, 678, 680, 699, 701, 729, 735, 740, 741, 746, 752, 753, 757, 759, 765, 771, 789, 795, 805, 815, 817, 821
Godhead 658, 668, 733, 777
heavens (see also 'sky') 535, 693, 736, 741, 745, 750, 754, 755, 758, 761, 775
light 627, 631, 683, 687, 688, 691, 694, 697, 699, 709, 744, 746, 747, 750, 752, 755, 760, 763, 764, 788, 795, 799, 807, 810
limit (see also 'boundary') 728, 732, 744, 825, 838
Lord 525, 595, 604, 800, 803, 806
Maker 529, 536, 544, 545, 697, 703, 727
making 534, 548, 652, 662
moon 796, 810, 813
morning 689, 724, 822, 825, 828, 838
Moses 737, 739
Most High 793
nature 591, 595, 602, 603
night 671, 672, 673, 679, 682, 685, 690, 696, 700, 702, 705, 708, 711, 713, 724, 730, 760, 762, 772, 780, 833, 834
Paul 692, 737, 749
roof 664

sea   570, 599, 600, 619, 639, 653, 657, 659, 744
shade   666
shadow   672, 673, 680, 685, 702, 757, 761, 762, 763, 772, 779, 781
signal   537, 551, 660, 662, 670, 751, 768
sky (see also 'heavens')   735, 753, 767, 771
Stephen   692
sun   628, 745, 796, 810, 813
tent   552, 665, 791

vault   669
water   521, 522, 549, 553, 554, 559, 561, 564, 566, 575, 577, 578, 579, 582, 583, 585, 586, 587, 589, 590, 594, 598, 601, 605, 606, 607, 608, 610, 611, 612, 613, 614, 616, 617, 624, 627, 635, 636, 637, 640, 641, 642, 643, 657, 661, 663, 683, 691, 731, 815, 821
wind   553, 611, 613, 616, 619, 620, 623, 626
wisdom   793, 811

INDEX OF BIBLICAL REFERENCES

Genesis
    1:1   739
    1:2   547, 553, 611, 823
    1:6   521–522, 530, 549, 577, 605, 740
    1:8   822
    1:12   803
    1:19   803
    1:21   803
    1: 25   803
    1: 31   803

Exodus
    3:14   540
    14:21   601
    17:6   601

Ezekiel
    1:26–28   692, 749

Acts of the Apostles
    7:55–56   692
    9:3   692, 749
    22:6   692, 749
    26:13   692, 749

www.ingramcontent.com/pod-product-compliance
Lightning Source LLC
Chambersburg PA
CBHW050141240426
43673CB00043B/1753